when we grow up

melanie walsh

When we
grow up ...

With thanks to Richard Scarry, who inspired
me to make books when I grew up.

First published 2020 by Walker Books Ltd
87 Vauxhall Walk, London SE11 5HJ

2 4 6 8 10 9 7 5 3 1

Copyright © 2020 Melanie Walsh

The right of Melanie Walsh to be identified as author/illustrator of
this work has been asserted by her in accordance with the Copyright,
Designs and Patents Act 1988

This book has been typeset in Helvetica Neue and WB Walsh

Printed in China

British Library Cataloguing in Publication Data:
a catalogue record for this book is available from the British Library

ISBN 978-1-4063-8781-0

www.walker.co.uk

WALKER BOOKS
AND SUBSIDIARIES
LONDON • BOSTON • SYDNEY • AUCKLAND

what can
we be?

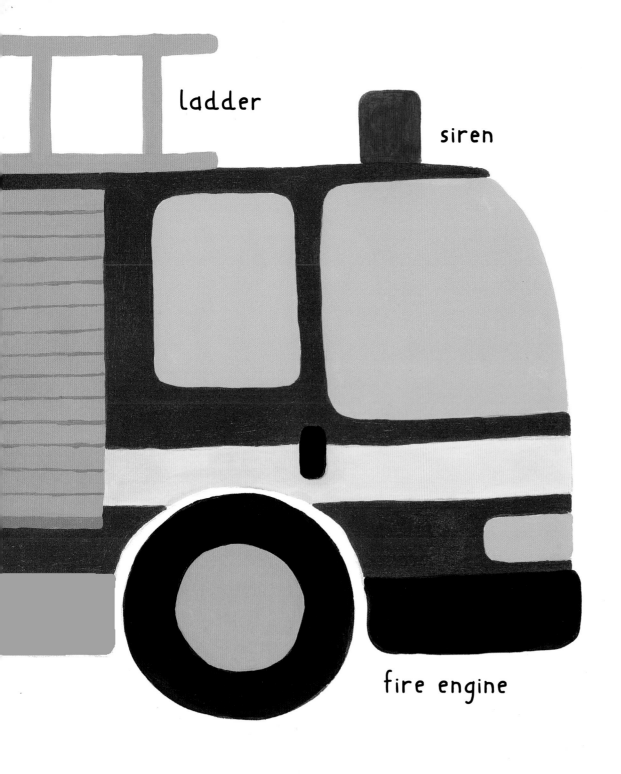

ladder

siren

fire engine

I can be a firefighter.

Firefighters put out fires and rescue pets.

helmet

visor

torch

cat

uniform

hose

I can be a vet.

Vets help ill and hurt animals.

stethoscope

bandage

X-ray

scrubs

scales

syringe

dog

wheel

overalls

I can be
a mechanic.

Mechanics fix cars and trucks.

oil

puncture

pliers   screwdriver

wrench

sockets

I can be a musician or a dancer.

Musicians play instruments and dancers perform to the music.

costume

stage

ballet shoes

I can be a teacher.

Teachers help children learn new things.

children

pencil

paper

ruler

whiteboard

story
book

mirror

water

gel

comb

I can be a hairdresser.
Hairdressers cut and style hair.

hairspray

hairdryer

scissors

I can be a doctor or a nurse.

Doctors and nurses look after sick
and injured people.

blood-pressure monitor

teddy

patient

thermometer

medicine

plaster cast

goal

goalkeeper gloves

pitch

football

shirt

boots

I can be a footballer.
Footballers play in a team to score goals.

I can be a builder.

Builders use bricks and wood
to make buildings.

trowel

hi-vis jacket

bricks

mortar

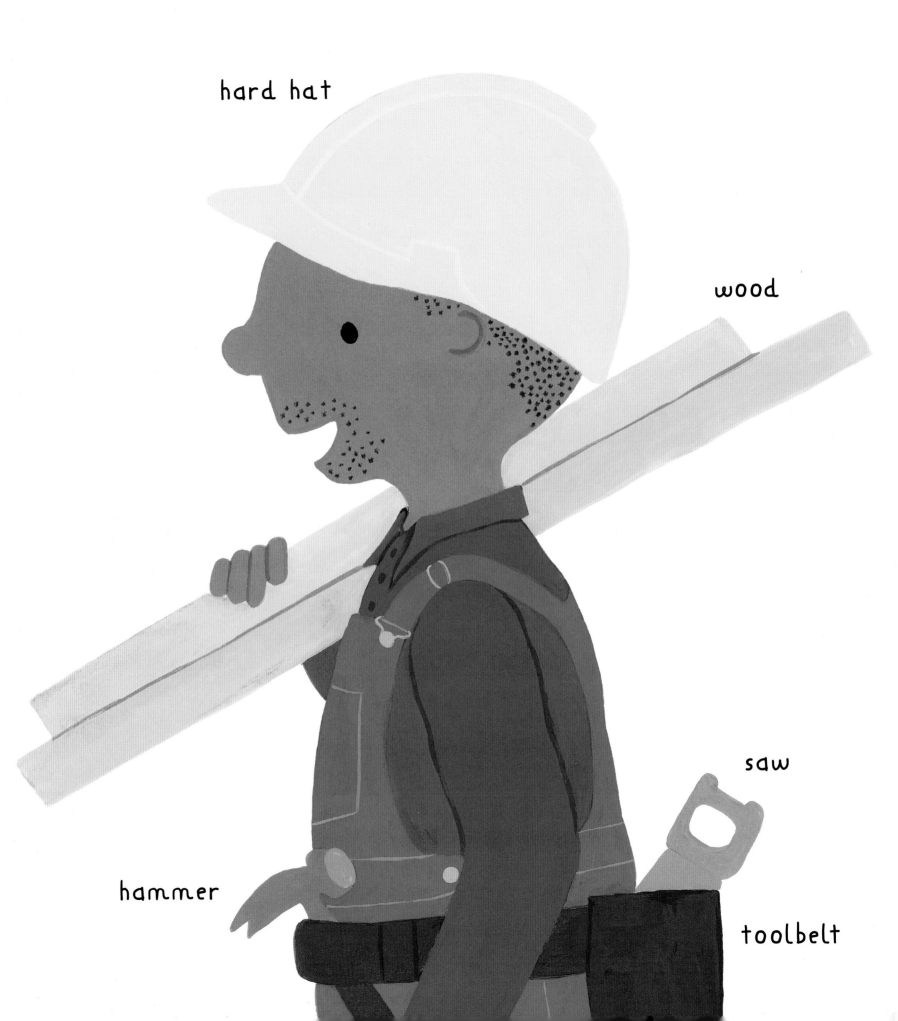

hard hat

wood

saw

hammer

toolbelt

I can be a programmer or an astronaut.

Programmers write instructions in code for computers to follow. Astronauts fly spacecrafts.

computer

headset

keyboard

teacher

doctor

firefighter

We can be anything we want!

builder

astronaut

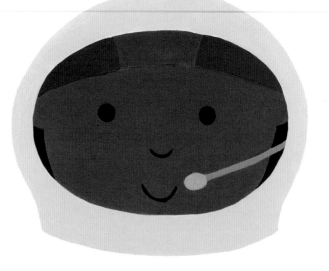

dancer

footballer

mechanic

What do you want to be when you grow up?

programmer

vet